Searchlight
BOOKS™

What's
Amazing
about Space?

Exploring
Space
Robots

Deborah Kops

Lerner Publications Company
Minneapolis

▶ For every reader who wants to explore space—with the help of a book, a telescope, or a robot.

Lerner Publications Company
A division of Lerner Publishing Group, Inc.
241 First Avenue North
Minneapolis, MN 55401 U.S.A.

Website address: www.lernerbooks.com

Library of Congress Cataloging-in-Publication Data

Kops, Deborah.
      Exploring space robots / by Deborah Kops.
          p.   cm. — (Searchlight Books™—What's amazing about space?)
      Includes index.
      ISBN 978-0-7613-5445-1 (lib. bdg. : alk. paper)
      1. Space robotics—Juvenile literature. I. Title.
   TL1097.K66 2012
   629.46—dc22   2010044213

Manufactured in the United States of America
1 – DP – 7/15/11

Contents

Chapter 1

ROBOTS ON
THE GO . . . **page 4**

Chapter 2

FAMOUS SPACE
ROBOTS . . . **page 10**

Chapter 3

ROBOTS AT WORK . . . **page 15**

Chapter 4

WHO CONTROLS SPACE ROBOTS? . . . **page 23**

Chapter 5

THE FUTURE OF SPACE ROBOTS . . . **page 31**

Glossary • 38
Learn More about Space Robots • 39
Index • 40

ROBOTS ON THE GO

A robot with six wheels drives to a rock. The robot is about the size of a golf cart. Its name is *Opportunity*. The rock and the robot are on the planet Mars.

Opportunity rolls across the surface of Mars. What does *Opportunity* do on Mars?

The rock is called Chocolate Hills. It is covered with dark stuff. The coating reminds scientists of chocolate. They want to know what that dark coating is. *Opportunity* explores Chocolate Hills.

Opportunity uses its instruments to find out what the coating is. Then the robot sends the information back to Earth. With *Opportunity*'s help, the scientists are learning about Mars.

Opportunity uses its robotic arm as it examines the surface of Mars.

What Are Space Robots?

A robot is a machine that performs tasks. People install computer programs in robots. These sets of instructions tell the robots what to do. Some robots work in space.

This image shows the robot *Spirit*, which went to Mars the same year as *Opportunity*.

Engineers prepare *Curiosity* for launch. This rover is bigger than *Opportunity*. It is designed to search for life on Mars.

Opportunity is a type of space robot called a rover. A rover moves around on wheels. It explores other worlds.

Rovers aren't the only types of space robots. Spacecraft called probes fly through space. Orbiters circle high above planets and moons. Other space robots fix spacecraft. Robots also deliver supplies to the International Space Station (ISS). That's a spacecraft where scientists live and work.

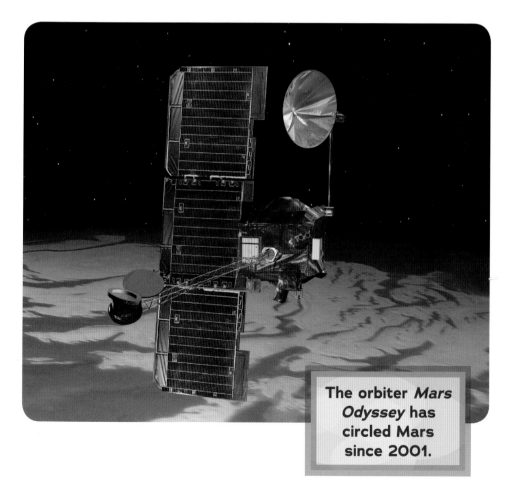

The orbiter *Mars Odyssey* has circled Mars since 2001.

Chapter 2

FAMOUS SPACE ROBOTS

The first rover in space traveled on the Moon. It was called *Lunokhod 1*. It drove on the Moon for eleven months. It had a video camera. *Lunokhod 1* sent thousands of pictures back to Earth.

Lunokhod 1 is shown here in 1970. What did *Lunokhod* explore?

Viking 1

Viking 1 gave Earth its first close look at Mars. *Viking 1* was really two space robots. It had an orbiter and a lander. The orbiter circled around Mars in space. The lander touched down on the surface of Mars. It had no wheels. So it stayed in one place.

The *Viking 1* spacecraft pictured here was the first space robot to land on Mars.

Viking 1 took this photo from the surface of Mars.

The *Viking 1* lander had a scoop. It picked up soil from Mars. Then it ran tests in its onboard laboratory. Scientists thought the lander might find tiny living things in the soil. But it didn't find any.

Robots in Deep Space

Voyager 1 and *Voyager 2* flew farther out into space.
The two probes visited Jupiter, Saturn, Neptune, and
Uranus. These planets are far from the Sun and Earth.

THE *VOYAGER* SPACECRAFT
WERE LAUNCHED IN 1977.

The Voyager mission probes took pictures of the planets. For the first time, people saw details of the planets. Both probes are still sending signals back to Earth.

Voyager 2 took this image of Neptune when it flew by the planet in 1989.

Chapter 3

ROBOTS AT WORK

This drawing shows a probe hitting the surface of the Moon. What did scientists hope to discover with this experiment?

Robots do many jobs in space. Some even crash on purpose! Scientists thought the Moon might have frozen water in one of its craters. So they had a probe smash into the crater. When the probe hit the crater, bits of ice flew out. It was the first time scientists found water on the Moon.

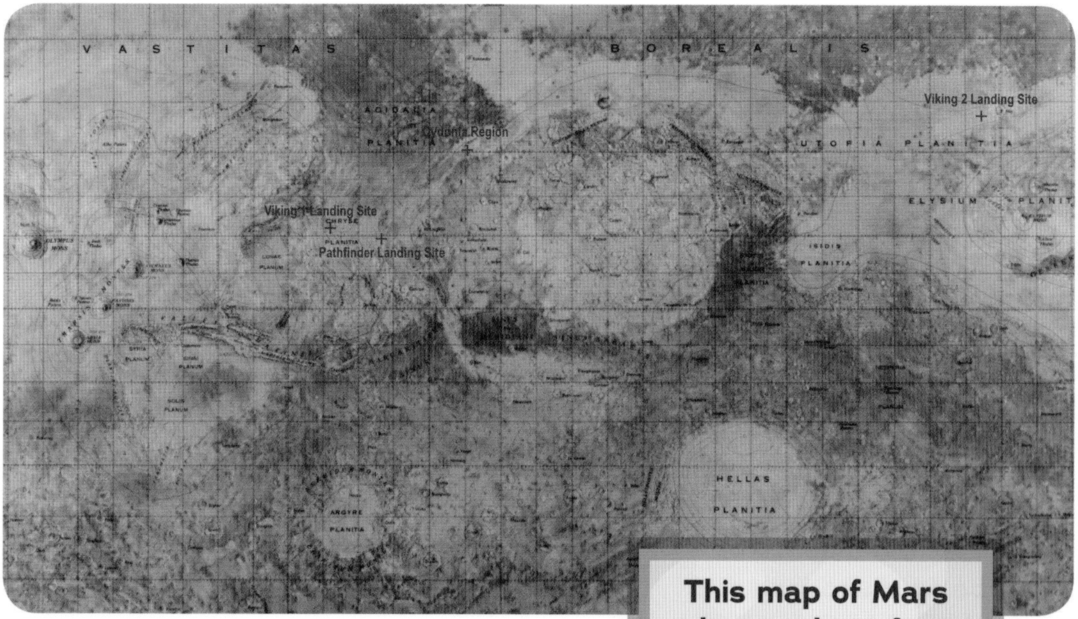
V A S T I T A S
B O R E A L I S
ACIDALIA
PLANITIA
Cydonia Region
Viking 2 Landing Site
UTOPIA PLANITIA
ELYSIUM
Viking 1 Landing Site
CHRYSE
PLANITIA
Pathfinder Landing Site
ISIDIS
PLANITIA
HELLAS
PLANITIA
ARGYRE
PLANITIA

This map of Mars shows where four robots have landed.

Mapping the Surface

Orbiters take pictures of a planet or a moon. Scientists can use the pictures to make maps of the surface. These maps may one day help people decide which parts of a planet to visit.

One orbiter that circles the Moon can record temperatures on the Moon's surface. This robot measured a temperature of –415°F (–248°C). That's the coldest temperature recorded on any moon or planet.

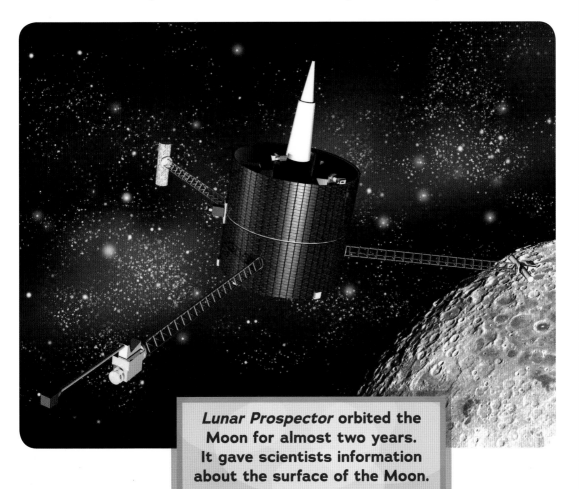

Lunar Prospector orbited the Moon for almost two years. It gave scientists information about the surface of the Moon.

Exploring

Robots can also drive on the surface of other worlds.
Rovers can go to places that are too dangerous for people.
They take pictures. They also run tests on rocks and soil.

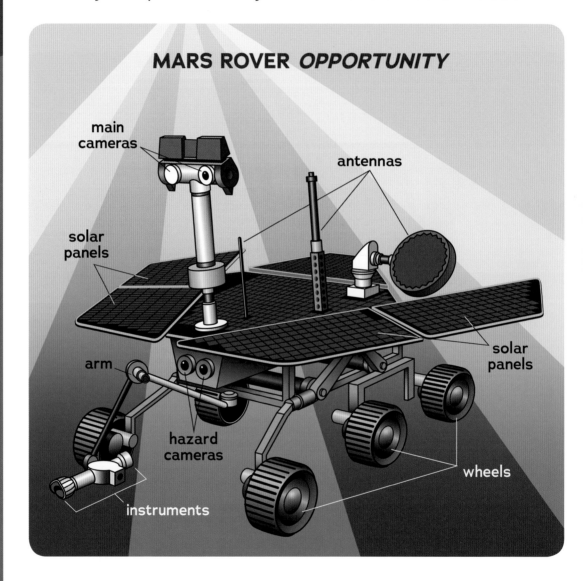

MARS ROVER *OPPORTUNITY*

main cameras

antennas

solar panels

solar panels

arm

hazard cameras

wheels

instruments

Scientists test the robotic arm on *Curiosity*.

A Mars rover named *Curiosity* has a drill. It can make a hole in a rock. The drill creates dust. *Curiosity* studies the dust to learn what the rock is made of.

A Russian spacecraft docks at the International Space Station to drop off supplies.

Robots at the International Space Station

Not all robots are for exploring. Some make deliveries. They are like giant delivery trucks in space. These robots are cargo ships. They bring supplies to the ISS.

Some cargo ships need help parking next to the ISS. A robot called Canadarm2 comes to the rescue. The giant robot arm reaches out and grabs cargo ships. Canadarm2 is huge. It's longer than a school bus!

An astronaut is attached to Canadarm2 while working outside the ISS.

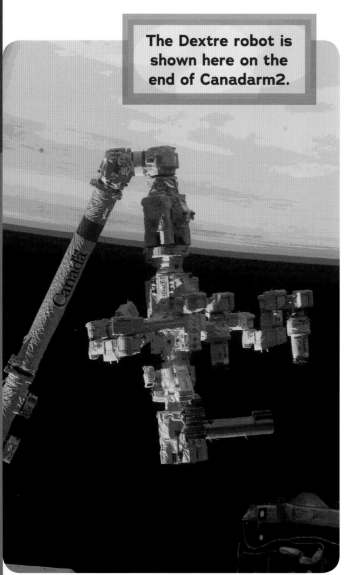

The Dextre robot is shown here on the end of Canadarm2.

Canada

Dextre is another robot on the ISS. Dextre is 12 feet (3.6 meters) tall. It has two arms. Each arm holds a wrench. Dextre uses its wrenches to grab objects. It can replace damaged parts. It can also move large objects.

Chapter 4

WHO CONTROLS SPACE ROBOTS?

Space robots need computer programs to run. But most robots also need the help of human controllers. The controllers give the robots directions.

A controller aboard a space shuttle operates a robotic arm. How do controllers help robots run?

An astronaut works
the controls of the
Canadarm2 inside the ISS.

For example, Canadarm2 can't catch a cargo ship by itself. It needs someone to run its controls. The controller tells Canadarm2 exactly what to do.

Not all cargo ships need help from people. Some have advanced programs. These programs allow the ships to park themselves. Controllers on Earth still keep track of these ships. They can take over control if there's a problem.

Controllers at the space center in Houston, Texas, use computers to track the ISS.

Opportunity's Drivers

No one drives *Opportunity* around Mars. But the rover communicates with its controllers on Earth. *Opportunity* explores all day. Then it sends pictures back to Earth. The rover turns itself off at night.

Opportunity took this photo of small, pea-sized rocks on the surface of Mars.

While the rover sleeps, scientists on Earth work. They study the pictures that *Opportunity* sent. They decide where to send the rover next. They send instructions to the rover. When *Opportunity* powers up, it knows what to do.

Controllers prepare for the rover *Spirit* to land on Mars.

Controlling Deep Space Probes

Probes that travel very far from Earth still receive commands from Earth. The probe *New Horizons* is zooming into deep space. It is going to a dwarf planet called Pluto. A dwarf planet is not quite big enough to be a planet. *New Horizons* will be the first probe to go to Pluto.

The *New Horizons* space probe takes off from the launchpad aboard a rocket.

New Horizons gets farther from Earth every day. Signals take a long time to go back and forth. The probe needs a strong antenna to send and receive signals.

New Horizons approaches Pluto and its three moons in this drawing.

On Earth, controllers
listen for signals from
New Horizons. They use
big, round antennas. The
biggest one is 230 feet
(70 m) across. That is
more than half the length
of a soccer field!

Chapter 5

THE FUTURE OF SPACE ROBOTS

Space robots teach us about the universe. They go to places where people cannot travel. Humans cannot go to Pluto. It is too far away. It would take an astronaut more than nine years to get there!

This drawing shows what Pluto might look like from its moon Charon. Can robots help us explore this distant world?

More Robots on Mars

Scientists are interested in Mars. Some of them believe that Mars may have once had life. The scientists want to study Mars to find out.

This photo shows Mars from space. Scientists hope to learn whether Mars once supported life.

ROBOTS CAN EXPLORE THE ROCKY
LAND ON THE SURFACE OF MARS.

But studying Mars is not easy. It is far from Earth. It is a dangerous place. Mars is too cold for people to live on its surface. People cannot breathe its air. That's why robots are important to studying Mars. They can work in the cold. They don't need any air.

In this drawing, the *Phoenix* Mars lander uses a laser beam to detect dust and clouds in the air.

Many more robots will go to Mars in the future. An orbiter will learn more about Mars's air. Another robot will be a laboratory on wheels. It will search areas where water once ran on Mars's surface. One day a robot may even be able to send some of Mars's rocks back to Earth!

New Frontiers

Space robots will continue to help scientists understand space. A spacecraft called *Juno* will study Jupiter. Scientists hope *Juno* will help them learn how Jupiter formed.

The *Juno* spacecraft flies past Jupiter in this drawing.

Another probe will travel close to the Sun. It will help scientists learn more about this star. The probe will need a special shield. The shield will protect it from the Sun's heat.

This drawing shows the *Solar Probe Plus* spacecraft gathering data on the Sun.

Space travel to places like Jupiter and the Sun is impossible for people. Even going to Mars would be very hard. Space robots are the only way we can learn about these exciting places.

A rocket blasts off from Mars in this illustration.

Glossary

antenna: a device that sends or receives radio signals

cargo ship: a robot that delivers supplies in space

computer program: a set of instructions that tells a robot what to do

crater: a bowl-shaped feature often formed when a space object hits a planet or a moon

dwarf planet: an object that circles the Sun and is not big enough to be classified as a planet

International Space Station (ISS): a spacecraft where scientists live and work

laboratory: an area set aside for scientific experiments

lander: a vehicle that lands on a planet or a moon

orbiter: a type of space robot that circles high above a planet or a moon

probe: a type of space robot that flies through space

robot: a machine that performs tasks with the help of computer programs

rover: a type of space robot that moves around on wheels

Learn More about Space Robots

Books

Hyland, Tony. *Space Robots*. North Mankato, MN: Smart Apple Media, 2008. Read about the past and future of space robots.

Jefferis, David. *Space Probes: Exploring Beyond Earth*. New York: Crabtree, 2009. Find out more about space probes, what they do, and their role in space exploration.

Waxman, Laura Hamilton. *Exploring the International Space Station*. Minneapolis: Lerner Publications Company, 2012. The International Space Station circles high above Earth. Read about its mission and the astronauts who work there.

Websites

NASA Space Place
http://spaceplace.jpl.nasa.gov/en/kids
Learn all about space and space missions at the Space Place. The website includes games, videos, projects you can try, and more.

New Horizons: NASA's Pluto-Kuiper Belt Mission
http://pluto.jhuapl.edu/education/students.php
Make your own Pluto globe or download a poster about the New Horizons space mission.

Solar System Exploration
http://solarsystem.nasa.gov/kids/index.cfm
At this site, you can find out what your weight would be on Mars or put together a puzzle about a planet.

Index

Curiosity, 19

Earth, 6, 10–11, 13–14, 25–30, 33–34

International Space Station (ISS), 9, 20–22

Juno, 35

landers, 11–12
Lunokhod 1, 10

Mars, 4, 6, 11–12, 19, 26, 32–34, 37
Moon, 10, 15, 17

New Horizons, 28–30

Opportunity, 4–6, 8, 26–27
orbiters, 9, 11, 16–17, 34

probes, 9, 13–15, 28–29, 36

rovers, 8–10, 18–19, 26–27

Sun, 13, 36–37

Viking 1, 11–12
Voyager 1, 13–14
Voyager 2, 13–14

Photo Acknowledgments

The images in this book are used with the permission of: NASA/JPL/Cornell University, pp. 4, 33; NASA/JPL-Caltech/Cornell, p. 5; NASA/JPL, pp. 6, 7, 9, 12, 13, 14, 16, 35, 37; NASA/JPL-Caltech, pp. 8, 19; © Keystone-France/Gamma-Keystone via Getty Images, p. 10; NASA, pp. 11, 20, 22, 24, 25, 34; NASA/Roger Arno, p. 15; NASA/GSFC, p. 17; © Laura Westlund/Independent Picture Service, p. 18; NASA/MSFC, p. 21; © AFP/Getty Images, p. 23; NASA/JPL/Cornell/USGS, p. 26; AP Photo/NASA, Bill Ingalls, p. 27; NASA/Kim Shiftlett, p. 28; NASA/JHUAPL/SwRI, p. 29; AP Photo/Neil Jacobs, p. 30; © Ron Miller, p. 31; NASA/JPL/MSSS, p. 32; JHU/APL, p. 36.
Front cover: NASA/JPL.

Main body text set in Adrianna Regular 14/20
Typeface provided by Chank